BATTLESHIP MISSOURI

359.3252
R769

Library of Congress Catalog Card
Number: 99-70720

First Printing, October 1999
1 2 3 4 5 6 7 8 9

Cover photos by Douglas Peebles
Design by Jane Hopkins
Previous page and these pages: The Battleship Missouri
Memorial in Pearl Harbor, Hawai'i

Softcover
ISBN 1-56647-252-0

Casebound
ISBN 1-56647-253-9

Mutual Publishing
1215 Center Street, Suite 210
Honolulu, Hawaii 96816
Ph: (808) 732-1709
Fax: (808) 734-4094
e-mail: mutual@lava.net
www.mutualpublishing.com

Printed in Taiwan

BATTLESHIP MISSOURI

The Battleship Missouri Memorial in Pearl Harbor, Hawai'i

Illustrated with Historic Photographs

Ronn Ronck

MUTUAL PUBLISHING

Mighty Mo

The USS *Missouri* (BB-63), the last battleship built by the United States, ruled the seas when she fired her nine 16-inch guns. Her lasting fame, however, rests not on her awesome firepower, but on her role as a peacemaker. It was on the *Missouri's* 01 deck that Japan formally surrendered to the Allied Powers on September 2, 1945, to end World War II.

Launched on January 29, 1944, at the New York Navy Yard, the 58,000-ton *Missouri* is 887 feet, three inches long and 108 feet, two inches wide. Powered by four giant turbine engines, the ship was capable of traveling at 33 knots. Its original World War II crew consisted of 134 officers and 2,400 enlisted personnel.

The battleship also served in the Korean War between 1950 and 1953 and, after reactivation and modernization, in the Persian Gulf War, 1990 to 1991. Decommissioned for the second time in 1992, the ship spent six years in mothballs before being released by the Navy in 1998 and towed to its permanent home in Pearl Harbor. The Battleship Missouri Memorial was opened to the public on January 29, 1999, exactly 55 years to the day after its initial launch.

Adm. Chester Nimitz

Gen. Douglas MacArthur

Allied Officers

Japanese Foreign Minister Mamoru Shigemitsu

Japanese Delegation

U. S. Officers

SURRENDER PARTICIPANTS, SEPTEMBER 2, 1945

Six-foot man shown to scale

Triple 16-inch gun turret No. 1. The measurement is based on the diameter of the barrel. Each gun can fire two rounds per minute and is capable of firing a 2,700-pound projectile 23 miles, roughly the distance between Honolulu and Waianae.

Teakwood deck. Will not rot if properly maintained.

Hull. The main armor belt of the hull is 13.5 inches thick.

Anchor chain is 1,080 feet long and each link weighs 120 pounds.

Anchor on port and starboard bow, each weighing 30,000 pounds.

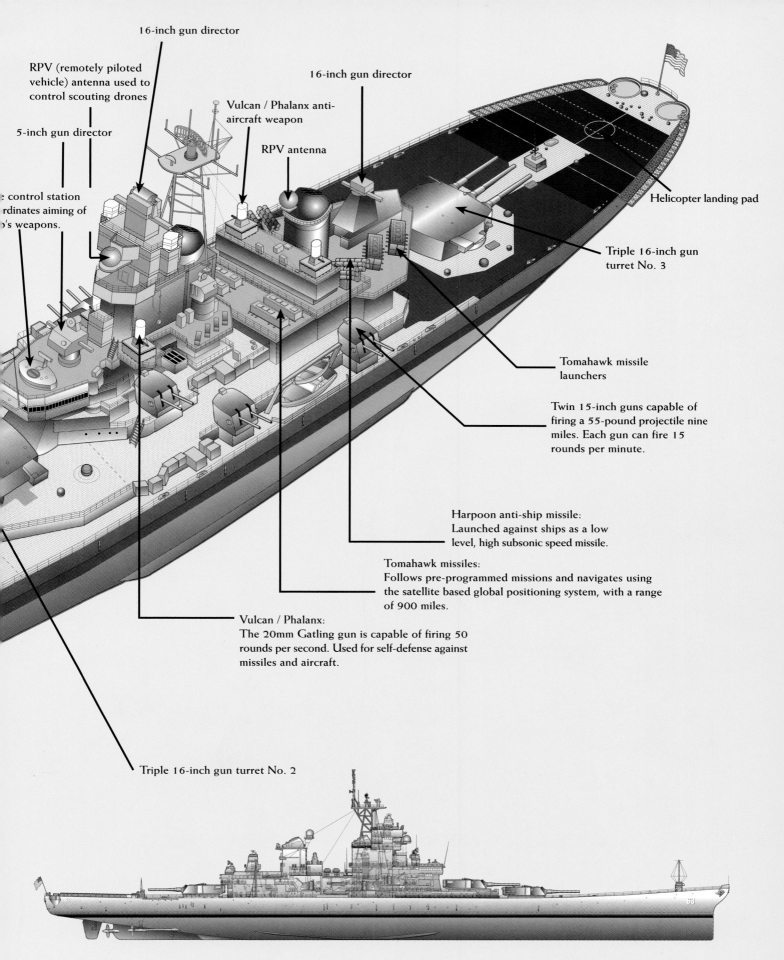

16-inch gun director

RPV (remotely piloted vehicle) antenna used to control scouting drones

5-inch gun director

e control station rdinates aiming of p's weapons.

16-inch gun director

Vulcan / Phalanx anti-aircraft weapon

RPV antenna

Helicopter landing pad

Triple 16-inch gun turret No. 3

Tomahawk missile launchers

Twin 15-inch guns capable of firing a 55-pound projectile nine miles. Each gun can fire 15 rounds per minute.

Harpoon anti-ship missile: Launched against ships as a low level, high subsonic speed missile.

Tomahawk missiles: Follows pre-programmed missions and navigates using the satellite based global positioning system, with a range of 900 miles.

Vulcan / Phalanx: The 20mm Gatling gun is capable of firing 50 rounds per second. Used for self-defense against missiles and aircraft.

Triple 16-inch gun turret No. 2

Graphics by David Swann, *Honolulu Star-Bulletin*

Table of Contents

▼ BELOW: The Battleship Missouri Memorial greets visitors in Pearl Harbor. A wraparound shield on the ship's bow originally protected 20mm guns. (DOUGLAS PEEBLES)

Welcome Aboard

➤ RIGHT: The *Missouri* participates in PacEx '89 battle group exercises en route to Korea in October 1989. Her sister battleship, the *New Jersey*, is beyond at left, and the aircraft carrier *Enterprise* is behind the foremast.(U.S. NAVAL INSTITUTE)

The USS *Missouri*, the last of America's great battleships, has a secure spot in military history. But, while the *Missouri* will always be remembered as the site where the Japanese formally surrendered to the Allies at the end of World War II, the bronze plaque mounted in the 01 deck tells only part of the story.

Commissioned in 1944, three years after its keel was laid in the New York Navy Yard, the *Missouri* joined the U.S. Pacific Fleet on its final drive toward Japan. Before the surrender, it supported the invasion of Iwo Jima and joined in shore strikes against Okinawa and Tokyo.

During the Korean War, it conducted shore bombardments against the North Koreans and Chinese and, during the Persian Gulf War, it helped to liberate Kuwait. During three wars, and a half-century of service, "Mighty Mo" symbolized our nation's strength and determination to build a better, more peaceful world.

The Battleship Missouri Memorial invites you to learn more about the *Missouri* and to experience what life was like for the officers and enlisted men who stood on her bridge, ate in her mess halls and fired her guns. Walk upon the upper deck and envision General MacArthur and the Foreign Minister of Japan sitting down here to sign the surrender papers that brought the fighting to an end.

As you tour this legendary battleship, you will also learn about today's U.S. Navy and its role in the world. Take your time and enjoy your visit to the *Missouri*. We are happy to have you aboard.

The Last Battleship

Enemy Threat

⚓

The Missouri's keel-laying ceremony, on January 6, 1941, was a closed military event and the building of the battleship was largely kept from pubic view. Naval officials worried that Germany might try to infiltrate the New York Navy Yard.

▲ ABOVE: The keel-laying ceremony for the *Missouri* was held on January 6, 1941, at the New York Navy Yard. Rear Admiral Clark Woodward, commandant of the Third Naval District, leans over to drive in the first rivet. (NATIONAL ARCHIVES)

To onlookers it appeared that Margaret Truman launched the USS *Missouri* all by herself. After christening the ship with a magnum of champagne on January 29, 1944, the 19-year-old daughter of senator and future President Harry S Truman gave the bow a playful shove and it slid down the runway of the New York Navy Yard into the East River.

Named after Truman's home state, the *Missouri* (BB-63), nicknamed the "Mighty Mo," was the last great battleship completed by the Navy. Its story began in 1938 when Congress, fearful of a two-ocean war, appropriated a billion dollars to expand the U.S. fleet. Nearly $115 million of this went to build the *Missouri*, whose 887-foot keel was laid 11 months before the Japanese dropped their bombs on Pearl Harbor.

Battleships, of course, aren't built in one day. Even with the highest government priority, it took thousands of patriotic shipyard workers three-and-a-half years to help the battleship grow to nearly the length of three football fields. Extra spaces in the blueprints were filled with the latest weapons, radar, and communications systems. When completed, the *Missouri* was a virtual city at sea, with its own post office, convenience stores, libraries, bakeries, barbershops, and laundries.

The *Missouri* is one of four great "Iowa-Class" battleships, along with the *Iowa, New Jersey* and *Wisconsin*. Magnificently designed, they were the fastest, best-protected and heaviest-armed battleships the world had ever seen. Intended for ship-to-ship gun battles, their strategic role changed after the attack on Pearl Harbor and they were then primarily used for ship-to-shore bombardment. A blast from the *Missouri's* powerful 16-inch guns could hit an enemy target 23 miles away.

While still under construction, 3,000 Navy officers applied for duty on the *Missouri*, more than 20 times its allotment. The original wartime crew eventually consisted of 134 officers and 2,400 enlisted men, many of whom had never been to sea before. Like most young recruits, they were expected to learn their skills on the job. Captain William M. Callaghan, a member of Admiral Chester Nimitz's staff in Hawai'i, was chosen to be the *Missouri's* first commanding officer.

During the ship's shakedown training period in the Atlantic, it was welcomed into the fleet by the Navy's two oldest battleships, the *Arkansas*, commissioned in 1912, and the *Texas*, commissioned in 1914. Both ships, although starting to show their age, had provided gunfire cover for the Allied D-Day invasion of Normandy in June 1944.

The *Missouri* passed through the Panama Canal in November 1944. It was a tight squeeze for the 108-foot, 2-inch-wide ship since the canal locks are only 110 feet wide. After entering the Pacific, the *Missouri* stopped first at San Francisco to be outfitted as a fleet flagship and then headed west from California to Hawai'i.

▼ BELOW: The *Missouri* fires its 16-inch guns during the ship's shake-down cruise in August 1944. Arthur Stratham, part of Commander Edward Steichen's combat photo group, took this dramatic shot showing six projectiles heading toward their target. (NATIONAL ARCHIVES)

BY THE NUMBERS

The Indiana *(BB-1), launched in 1893, was the first modern U.S. battleship. At the start of World War II, there were 17 battleships in the fleet but three of these—the* Arizona, Utah *and the* Oklahoma*—were lost in the attack on Pearl Harbor. By the end of the war, there were 23 active battleships. although the* Wisconsin *(BB-64) was begun after the Battleship* Missouri *(BB-63) and has a higher hull number, the Battleship* Missouri *took three months longer to build and was the last battleship completed by the Navy.*

▲ ABOVE, TOP: Margaret Truman prepares to christen the *Missouri* on January 29, 1944, with a bottle of champagne. Watching, from left to right, are Rear Admiral Monroe Kelly, commandant of the New York Navy Yard; Rear Admiral Sherman S. Kennedy, and Margaret's father, U.S. Senator Harry S. Truman. (NATIONAL ARCHIVES)   ▲ BOTTOM: The launching of the *Missouri* was a major media event. Newsreel camera crews and still photographers crowd the press box platform. (NATIONAL ARCHIVES)   ➤ OPPOSITE PAGE: Two of the *Missouri's* eight boilers are shown in this progress photo taken July 3, 1942. The camera was pointed forward from about the middle of the ship. (NATIONAL ARCHIVES)

N.Y. JULY 8-42
URI (BB 63)
FORWARD FROM ABOUT AMIDSHIPS

Iowa-Class

⚓

Battleship Missouri is one of four Iowa-class battleships built during World War II. The model for the class was the Iowa, *followed by the* New Jersey, Wisconsin *and* Missouri. *Two others, the* Illinois *and* Kentucky *were begun but never completed. A larger group of battleships, the Montana-class, never got off the drawing board.*

▲ ABOVE, TOP: The *Missouri* (left) moves alongside the *Iowa* off the coast of Japan on August 20, 1945. The *Missouri* transferred 200 men over to her sister battleship for temporary duty with the Tokyo landing force. (NATIONAL ARCHIVES) ▲ BOTTOM: On October 15, 1945, the *Missouri* approaches the Miraflores locks (top) of the Panama Canal. The fit was so tight that the ship scraped the sides of the concrete docks. (NATIONAL ARCHIVES) ◄ OPPOSITE PAGE, TOP: The *Missouri* is commissioned at the New York Navy Yard on June 11, 1944. Future crew members and their families were invited to the ceremony placing the ship into active service. (NATIONAL ARCHIVES) ◄ BOTTOM: Two weeks after its commissioning, the *Missouri* rests below a crane in the New York Navy Yard. The ship was originally painted with a "dazzle" camouflage pattern of black, white and gray shapes designed to make it a more difficult target for submarines. (NATIONAL ARCHIVES)

Parts & Labor

The Battleship Missouri cost nearly $115 million to build in the 1940s, or more than $2 billion in today's dollars. Construction required four million feet of welding seams, a million rivets, 300 miles of wiring, 90 miles of pipe and 15,000 valves. It is unlikely that any sailor ever passed through each of its 852 manholes, 844 doors and 144 hatches.

The *Missouri* passes through the Panama Canal for the last time on December 9, 1986. The locks are only slightly wider than the ship. (U.S. NAVAL INSTITUTE)

World War II

The *Missouri* made its first visit to Pearl Harbor on Christmas Eve 1944, when the battleship reported for duty with the Pacific Fleet. All hands stood on deck as it solemnly passed the ghostly wreck of the battleship USS *Arizona*, which had been sunk during the surprise Japanese air attack on December 7, 1941.

After the *Missouri* delivered its mailbags full of holiday mail, it continued westward to the Caroline Islands in Micronesia, where it joined the American armada operating out of Ulithi Lagoon. The Navy's Pacific Fleet, having leapfrogged through the Pacific Islands, was now posed to attack the Japanese mainland. During the early months of 1945, the *Missouri* supported aircraft carrier strikes against Tokyo and Iwo Jima in the Bonin Islands, and participated in the shore bombardment of Okinawa.

Part of the *Missouri*'s combat mission was also to serve as a refueling ship for the Navy's speedy destroyers. These vulnerable "tin cans," less than half the size of the *Missouri*, provided antiaircraft and antisubmarine protection for the fleet but had limited oil storage capacity. It was not unusual during this time for the *Missouri* to refuel four destroyers at once.

One of the destroyers refueled by the *Missouri* was the USS *Callaghan*. She was named after Rear Admiral Daniel J. Callaghan, killed on the bridge of his flagship during the first naval battle of Guadalcanal. His younger brother, Captain William M. Callaghan, now stood on the bridge of the *Missouri*.

The *Missouri*, along with the *New Jersey* and *Wisconsin*, opened fire on the Okinawan coast in late March. Their 16-inch guns knocked out shore batteries, antiaircraft installations, barracks and an ammunition storage depot. The bombardment eventually forced the enemy back from the shoreline.

On Easter Sunday, April 1, 1945, the invasion of Okinawa threw Japan into fits of desperation. It attacked the United States fleet with a massive counterattack of kamikaze planes that sank three ships and damaged many others. On April 11, a suicide plane crashed into the starboard hull of the *Missouri*, scattering wreckage on the upper deck.

The *Missouri* lowered its American flag to half-mast a day later, April 12, upon being notified of the death of President Franklin D. Roosevelt. Vice-president Harry S Truman, selected by Roosevelt as his running mate in the last election, was sworn in as the 33rd president of the United States.

By the late summer of 1945, the worst was over. The *Missouri*, now flagship of Admiral William F. "Bull" Halsey, commander of the Navy's Third Fleet, encountered little opposition during its bombardment of Hokkaido and Honshu in July. On August 6 the first atomic bomb was dropped on Hiroshima, and three days later a second bomb was dropped on Nagasaki. President Truman announced on August 14 that Japan had accepted defeat.

Fire Away

The seas shook whenever the Battleship Missouri fired its big 16-inch guns. There are two turrets of three guns each in front of the ship and a third turret of three guns in back. This placement allowed the ship to fire six guns at a target ahead, three astern and nine to either side. Each of the battleship's guns can fire a 2,700-pound projectile 23 miles.

▲ ABOVE: In July 1945 the *Missouri* tests her 16-inch guns before beginning the bombardment of Japan's home islands. The principal targets were industrial facilities on Hokkaido and Honshu. (NATIONAL ARCHIVES) ◄ OPPOSITE PAGE: The *Missouri* anchors off Guam in May 1945 to take aboard Admiral William F. Halsey, the new commander of the Third Fleet. In the background are two escort carriers and a hospital ship. (NATIONAL ARCHIVES)

Tora! Tora! Tora!

On the morning of December 7, 1941, there were about 100 Navy ships present in Pearl Harbor. Eight were battleships and the rest were cruisers, destroyers and support ships.

Half of the Pacific Fleet was out to sea or moored elsewhere, including its three aircraft carriers. The Enterprise was 200 miles west of Pearl Harbor, the Lexington was 425 miles southeast of Midway, and the Saratoga was being overhauled in San Diego.

The Japanese task force was disappointed that the carriers were not present but decided to go ahead with the attack and target the battleships instead. At 6 a.m. they launched the first of two waves of 353 fighters and dive bombers from six of their own carriers about 230 miles north of O'ahu.

When it became clear that the attack was a surprise, the prearranged victory call, "Tora! Tora! Tora!," was transmitted by radio back to the enemy fleet. Two minutes later the first bombs began to fall.

All of the battleships were damaged by bombs and aerial torpedoes. Five were sunk. Eleven other ships were heavily damaged, two beyond repair.

A total of 188 planes were also destroyed on the ground and another 159 damaged. The Japanese lost only 29 aircraft.

In time, however, the crippled Pearl Harbor fleet came back to life. The Arizona and the Utah were the only complete losses among the battleships. The California, Nevada and Virginia were raised, modernized and returned to service.

The 20 Japanese ships that had participated in the Pearl Harbor air raid shared the same fate as their country. They were all lost during the war.

U.S. Navy Ships Present at Pearl Harbor
December 7, 1941, 8 a.m.

Battleships (BB)
Pennsylvania (BB-38) [In dry-dock #1.]
Arizona (BB-39) [Sunk. Below the Arizona Memorial]
Nevada (BB-36) [Sunk. Raised, rebuilt and returned to service.]
Oklahoma (BB-37) [Sunk. Raised but not rebuilt.]
Tennessee (BB-43)
California (BB-44) [Sunk. Raised, rebuilt and returned to service.]
Maryland (BB-46)
West Virginia (BB-48) [Sunk. Raised, rebuilt and returned to service.]

Heavy Cruisers (CA)
New Orleans (CA-32)
San Francisco (CA-38)

Light Cruisers (CL)
Raleigh (CL-7)
Detroit (CL-8)
Phoenix (CL-46)
Honolulu (CL-48)
St. Louis (CL-49)
Helena (CL-50)

Destroyers (DD)
Allen (DD-66)
Schley (DD-103)
Chew (DD-106)
Ward (DD-139) [Patrolling entrance to Pearl Harbor.]
Farragut (DD-348)
Dewey (DD-349)
Hull (DD-350)
MacDonough (DD-351)
Worden (DD-352)
Dale (DD-353)
Monaghan (DD-354)
Aylwin (DD-355)
Selfridge (DD-357)
Phelps (DD-360)
Cummings (DD-365)
Reid (DD-369)
Case (DD-370)
Conyngham (DD-371)
Cassin (DD-372) [In dry-dock #1. Wrecked. Not rebuilt.]
Shaw (DD-373) [In floating dry-dock #2. Heavily damaged. Returned to service.]
Tucker (DD-374)
Downes (DD-375) [In dry-dock #1. Wrecked. Not rebuilt.]
Bagley (DD-386)

Blue (DD-387)
Helm (DD-388)
Mugford (DD-389)
Ralph Talbot (DD-390)
Henley (DD-391)
Patterson (DD-392)
Jarvis (DD-393)

Submarines (SS)
Narwhal (SS-167)
Dolphin (SS-169)
Cachalot (SS-170)
Tautog (SS-199)

Minelayer (CM)
Oglala (CM-4) [Sunk. Raised but not rebuilt.]

Minesweeper (AM)
Turkey (AM-13)
Bobolink (AM-20)
Rail (AM-26)
Tern (AM-31)
Grebe (AM-43)
Vireo (AM-52)

Coastal Minesweeper (AMc)
Cockatoo (AMc-8)
Crossbill (AMc-9)

Condor (AMc-14)
Reedbird (AMc-30)

Destroyer Minelayer (DM)
Gamble (DM-15)
Ramsay (DM-16)
Montgomery (DM-17)
Breese (DM-18)
Tracy (DM-19)
Preble (DM-20)
Sicard (DM-21)
Pruitt (DM-22)

Destroyer Minesweeper (DMS)
Zane (DMS-14)
Wasmuth (DMS-15)
Trever (DMS-16)
Perry (DMS-17)

Patrol Gunboat (PG)
Sacramento (PG-19)

Destroyer Tender (AD)
Dobbin (AD-3)
Whitney (AD-4)

U.S. Navy Ships Present at Pearl Harbor

Seaplane Tender (AV)
Curtiss (AV-4)
Tangier (AV-8)

Small Seaplane Tender (AVP)
Avocet (AVP-4)
Swan (AVP-7) [On marine railway dock.]

Seaplane Tender, Destroyer (AVD)
Hulbert (AVD-6)
Thornton (AVD-11)

Ammunition Ship (AE)
Pyro (AE-1)

Oiler (AO)
Ramapo (AO-12)
Neosho (AO-23)

Repair Ship (AR)
Medusa (AR-1)
Vestal (AR-4)
Rigel (AR-11)

Submarine Tender (AS)
Pelias (AS-14)

Submarine Rescue Ship (ASR)
Widgeon (ASR-1)

Hospital Ship (AH)
Solace (AH-5)

Cargo Ship (AK)
Vega (AK-17) [In Honolulu Harbor.]

Stores Issue Ship (AKS)
Castor (AKS-1)
Antares (AKS-3) [At entrance to Pearl Harbor.]

Ocean Tug (AT)
Ontario (AT-13)
Sunnadin (AT-28)
Keosanqua (AT-38) [At entrance of Pearl Harbor.]
Navajo (AT-64) [Twelve miles from Pearl Harbor entrance.]

Miscellaneous Auxiliary (AG)
Utah (AG-16) [Sunk. Never raised. Former battleship (BB-31) converted to targetship.]
Argonne (AG-31)
Sumner (AG-32)

▲ ABOVE: Navy photographer Len Schmidt took this shot of a Japanese kamikaze aircraft seconds before the fighter's left wing struck the hull of the *Missouri* on April 11, 1945. Crew members operate 40mm gun turrets in the foreground. (NATIONAL ARCHIVES)

Kamikaze Attack

While most Japanese kamikaze attacks during World War II were directed at aircraft carriers, these suicide planes sometimes took aim at other targets. On April 11, 1945, a kamikaze eluded the Battleship Missouri and struck the ship just below the main deck on the starboard side. The pilot was killed instantly and parts of the plane landed on the ship. The next day the crew held a military funeral for the enemy pilot and his remains were buried at sea.

▼ Below: A repair party stands on a wing of the enemy plane that landed on the starboard deck. The bomb aboard the kamikaze did not explode on impact and fell with parts of the plane into the ocean. (NATIONAL ARCHIVES)

➤ OPPOSITE PAGE, TOP: Bursts of flak darken the sky as a Japanese aircraft is shot down off the bow of the *Missouri* in April 1945. This photo was taken from the carrier *Intrepid.* (NATIONAL ARCHIVES) ➤ MIDDLE: When the kamikaze crashed into the *Missouri,* one of its forward mounted machine guns pierced a 40mm gun barrel. (NATIONAL ARCHIVES) ➤ BOTTOM: After military honors, the remains of the kamikaze pilot are buried at sea. Like many Japanese suicide pilots, he was still in his teens.
(NATIONAL ARCHIVES)

Crashing the Waves

The maximum draft of the Battleship Missouri, at full load, was 37 feet, nine inches. Smashing through the waves eliminated the pitch-and-roll common on smaller ships in the fleet but it caused topside problems in typhoon weather. Unexpectedly high waves were capable of washing away anything loosely stored on the decks.

Zeke Fighter

The kamikaze that struck the Missouri was a Mitsubishi Zero Sen A6M, given the code name "Zeke" by the Allies. It was the best fighter at the beginning of World War II and one of the attack planes that swooped down over Pearl Harbor. Its long range, superior maneuverability and rapid rate of climb were unmatched until later in the war.

Full-speed Ahead

⚓

Although blessed with great firepower and a heavy suit of armor, the Missouri *remained useful for a half-century because of its speed. Operating at a top speed of 33 knots, it was able to keep up with the fastest ships of the United States fleet through the Persian Gulf War. The Iowa-class battleships were the fastest battleships ever built.*

➤ RIGHT, TOP: An oil tanker, in foreground, refuels the *Missouri* at sea. Bombs and drums of lube oil are lashed to the deck of the tanker. (NATIONAL ARCHIVES)

▼ BOTTOM, LEFT: A Curtiss SC-1 Seahawk is lowered onto one of the *Missouri*'s fantail catapults. Floatplanes were used to spot and direct the battleship's artillery. (NATIONAL ARCHIVES)

▼ RIGHT: Crew members watch an evening boxing match on the fantail. In the background, a floatplane sits on its catapult. (NATIONAL ARCHIVES)

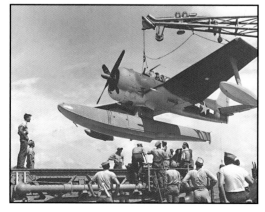

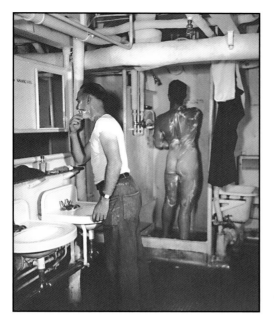

▲ ABOVE, TOP LEFT: One crew member shaves while another showers. Privacy was limited below decks on the *Missouri*. (NATIONAL ARCHIVES) ▲ TOP RIGHT: All of the chairs are taken in the ship's barbershop. During wartime, the bunkbeds folded up against the wall at left provided additional sleeping spaces. (NATIONAL ARCHIVES) ▲ BOTTOM: Pastry cooks scoop lemon filling for pies out of a mixing pot. The kitchen worked nearly around the clock to feed the crew. (NATIONAL ARCHIVES)

Wartime Hawai'i

▲ ABOVE: Thousands of American servicemen passed through Hawai'i, or were stationed here, during World War II. Many had their photographs taken with military buddies. (BAKER-VAN DYKE COLLECTION)

➤ OPPOSITE PAGE: The *Missouri* took its shakedown training cruise from New York to Norfolk, Virginia, in the summer of 1944. For many of the young crew members, this was their first sea duty. (NATIONAL ARCHIVES)

Life changed quickly in Hawai'i after Japan attacked Pearl Harbor on December 7, 1941. Although local residents were aware that the United States was balancing on the brink of World War II, they were still unprepared for the daring air raid and the impact war would bring to the islands.

The Japanese bombing run lasted less than two hours, from about 8 a.m. to 9:45 a.m., but the loss was great. More than 2,400 military and civilians were killed and the U.S. Pacific Fleet was devastated. Nearly half of the military deaths were men aboard the battleship USS *Arizona*, which sank just nine minutes after taking a direct hit in its forward powder magazine.

Hawai'i turned over its territorial government to the Army that afternoon. Military officials declared martial law and took control of the police and fire departments, public works, utilities, airports and the court system. Punahou School was commandeered the next day and turned into an Army base for the duration of the war.

Aloha Tower was painted with camouflage and barbed wire was strung along the shoreline and beaches. A curfew and blackout was imposed after dark. Civilians were fingerprinted, given a gas mask and issued an identification card.

Every household was asked to construct its own bomb shelter, and air raid trenches were scooped out of school yards and around public buildings. Bishop Museum and the Honolulu Academy of Arts moved their priceless collections into storage and banks shipped copies of their financial records to the mainland.

Hawai'i's population doubled to more than a million during the early 1940s, as waves of soldiers and sailors passed through to serve in the Pacific. Schofield Barracks on O'ahu, the Army's largest combat training base, became famous as the setting for James Jones' novel, *From Here to Eternity*, and its film version.

Parts of Honolulu took on a honky-tonk atmosphere of bars, cafes, souvenir shops and pleasure palaces. The Moana and Royal Hawaiian hotels in Waikiki, along with Fort De Russy, were used by the military for rest and relaxation. USO Clubs were opened throughout the islands.

The Battle of Midway, in June 1942, stopped the Japanese fleet's advance through the Pacific and essentially ended the direct threat to Hawai'i. The war dragged on for another three years until August 14, 1945, when the Japanese agreed to surrender. Peace returned to Hawai'i but the attack on Pearl Harbor, and its pivotal role during World War II, had changed it forever. On August 21, 1959, the former U.S. Territory of Hawai'i officially became the nation's 50th state.

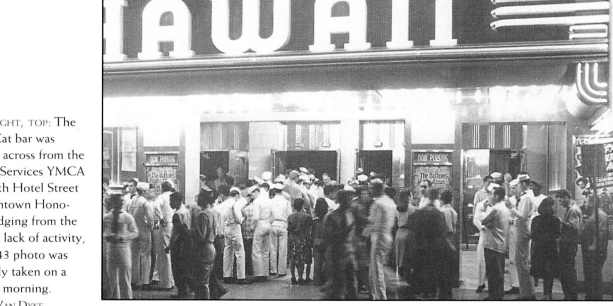

➤ RIGHT, TOP: The Black Cat bar was located across from the Armed Services YMCA on South Hotel Street in downtown Honolulu. Judging from the unusual lack of activity, this 1943 photo was probably taken on a Sunday morning. (BAKER-VAN DYKE COLLECTION)

➤ RIGHT, BOTTOM: A crowd of sailors outside the Hawaii Theatre entrance on Bethel Street in 1943. This historic landmark in downtown Honolulu has been recently restored. (BAKER-VAN DYKE COLLECTION)

Victory Gardens

During World War II, home-front gardeners produced an estimated 50 percent of America's vegetables. After the wife of Hawai'i's governor planted a vegetable garden on the grounds of Washington Place, others took up the challenge. More than 25,000 backyard gardens were established throughout the islands and large community gardens were established in parks, school yards and empty lots.

▲ ABOVE: An army camp looks abandoned at the foot of Nu'uanu Pali in 1945. During the war dozens of temporary Army bases were built on O'ahu. (BAKER-VAN DYKE COLLECTION) ◄ LEFT: Three sailors pose together in a Honolulu photo studio. Their smiling faces mask the uncertain future they would soon be facing out at sea. (BAKER-VAN DYKE COLLECTION)

➤ RIGHT: A wartime rendezvous in Honolulu provides an opportunity for a portrait. Military men often visited the photography studio at the urging of their parents, wives and girlfriends. (BAKER-VAN DYKE COLLECTION)

Working Women

⚓

Everyone had a job to do in wartime Hawai'i. When thousands of men joined the military and left for training and assignments, women took their positions. In addition to traditional female occupations such as clerks and typists, they went to work for factories, shipyards, and repair shops. Many others volunteered for the Red Cross or assisted in USO activities.

▲ ABOVE: A veteran Navy officer, local hula performers, and an Army sergeant of possible Japanese ancestry. While they recall the human face of World War II, their names were lost in the years that followed. (BAKER-VAN DYKE COLLECTION)

Japanese Citizens

There were 150,000 resident Japanese in Hawai'i at the start of the war and several hundred were arrested and questioned about their activities. Most were found to be trustworthy citizens. The Army's Japanese-American 100th Infantry Battalion and 442nd Regimental Combat Team, which fought in Europe, became the most decorated units of their size in American military history. Other Japanese-American men joined the U.S. Military Intelligence Service and accompanied regular troops to China, Burma and the Pacific Islands.

Japan Surrenders

Within days after President Truman announced that the war was over, it was decided that the formal Japanese surrender would take place aboard the *Missouri* in Tokyo Bay. The crew began cleaning, painting and polishing the Third Fleet flagship for the ceremony that took place on September 2, 1945.

Early that morning the blue-gray decks received a final scrubbing with fresh water, and a long table covered with a green cloth from the wardroom was set up on the starboard side of the veranda deck. The first visitors arrived at 7 a.m., when a destroyer pulled up alongside the *Missouri* and unloaded 150 reporters, photographers, cameramen and radio broadcasters. The ceremony was broadcast live over radio in the United States.

Crew members not on duty were allowed to find any spot they could to watch the ceremony. For many sailors and marines aboard the *Missouri*, this would be the most remembered day of their lives.

Fleet Admiral Chester W. Nimitz and General of the Army Douglas MacArthur were waiting in Admiral Halsey's cabin when the Japanese delegation, led by Foreign Minister Mamoru Shigemitsu, came aboard at 8:55 a.m. They were given a salute on deck by eight sideboys, the tallest sailors among the crew, who had

▲ ABOVE: General of the Army Douglas MacArthur and Fleet Admiral Chester W. Nimitz walk side-by-side toward the surrender table. Commander William Kitchell, flag lieutenant to Admiral William F. Halsey, walks ahead, while Halsey himself follows behind.
(NATIONAL ARCHIVES)

been selected for their height to impress the smaller Japanese.

In addition to Shigemitsu, the Japanese delegation consisted of two other members of the Foreign Office, six military officers and two government bureaucrats. They took their places in three rows facing the surrender table. On the bridge in front of them were painted eleven small "rising sun" flags. Each represented one of their country's aircraft shot down by the *Missouri*.

MacArthur opened the proceedings with a speech that expressed "the hope of all mankind that from this solemn occasion a better world shall merge" and that he would enforce the terms of the surrender with "justice and tolerance." This was welcome news for the Japanese, who had feared that the Allies would seek a victory of vengeance.

Shigemitsu then sat down, took off his top hat, and signed the surrender document at 9:04 a.m. He was followed over the next half-hour by General Yoshijiro Umezu of the Imperial General Staff, MacArthur, Nimitz, and representatives of the other Allied nations. When everyone had finished signing the document, MacArthur concluded the proceedings by saying, "let us pray that peace be now restored to the world and that God will preserve it always."

A few minutes later hundreds of planes from nearby aircraft carriers flew low over the *Missouri* to give the Japanese delegation a glimpse of their future. The American sleeping tiger had come roaring back after the tragic attack on Pearl Harbor and now controlled the destiny of their country.

Fixed Position

The exact position of the Battleship Missouri during the surrender ceremony is a matter of historical record. At precisely 9 a.m. the ship's navigators took bearings on six differernt objects from the bridge and established a precise fix. The electrical power to the gyrocompasses was then cut off so that no one else could claim a more accurate bearing at the exact time of signing. The position fixed was 35° 21' 17" north latitude and 139° 45' 36" east longitude.

▲ ABOVE: During the surrender ceremony, a low-flying Army plane shot this photo of crew members gathered on the deck of the Missouri. (NATIONAL ARCHIVES)

210624-S

Dressing Down

There was considerable discussion about how the crew would dress for the surrender ceremony. Some officers thought the uniform should be formal, while others preferred to attend the signing as they had fought. Admiral Nimitz decided that the officers and chiefs would wear khakis without neckties and the enlisted men would wear undress whites.

◄ OPPOSITE PAGE: Crew members perch wherever they can to get a glimpse of history. Small "rising sun" flags painted on the bridge represent enemy aircraft shot down in combat. The historic U.S. flag at lower right, framed backwards, was flown in 1853 by Commodore Perry at Tokyo Bay. (NATIONAL ARCHIVES) ◄ LEFT, TOP: Foreign Minister Mamoru Shigemitsu, with cane, stands in the front row of the Japanese delegation. Beside him is General Yoshijiro Umezu of the Imperial General Staff. (NATIONAL ARCHIVES)
◄ BOTTOM: Navy sideboys salute Foreign Minister Mamoru Shigemitsu, in top hat, as he prepares to step aboard. Marines watch in the foreground. (NATIONAL ARCHIVES)

➤ RIGHT, TOP: This bronze plaque marks the location of the surrender table on deck. It was designed and cast by workers in the Norfolk Navy Yard. (NATIONAL ARCHIVES)

➤ BOTTOM, LEFT: General Douglas MacArthur signs the surrender document for the Allied Powers. Behind him, left to right, are Lieutenant General Jonathan M. "Skinny" Wainright and General Sir Archibald Percival, both of whom had been prisoners of war. (NATIONAL ARCHIVES)

➤ BOTTOM, RIGHT: Sailors look down on the surrender table as the ceremony is about to end. From beginning to end, the signing ceremony lasted less than a half-hour. (NATIONAL ARCHIVES)

U.S.S. MISSOURI

OVER THIS SPOT
ON 2 SEPTEMBER 1945
THE INSTRUMENT
OF FORMAL SURRENDER
OF JAPAN TO THE ALLIED POWERS
WAS SIGNED
THUS BRINGING TO A CLOSE
THE SECOND WORLD WAR
——————
THE SHIP AT THAT TIME
WAS AT ANCHOR
IN TOKYO BAY

LATITUDE 35° 21' 17" NORTH ~ LONGITUDE 139° 45' 36" EAST

Japanese Representative

*The Japanese government sent Mamoru Shigemitsu, minister of foreign affairs,
to lead its official 110-man delegation aboard the Battleship Missouri. He had a wooden left leg
that slowed down his walk and banged against the surrender table as he took off his top hat
and sat down to sign the documents. It was later learned that Shigemitsu had worked
behind the scenes in Japan to end the war.*

INSTRUMENT OF SURRENDER

We acting by command of and in behalf of the Emperor of Japan, the Japanese Government and the Japanese Imperial General Headquarters, hereby accept the provisions set forth in the declaration issued by the heads of the Governments of the United States, China and Great Britain on 26 July 1945, at Potsdam, and subsequently adhered to by the Union of Soviet Socialist Republics, which four powers are hereafter referred to as the Allied Powers.

We hereby proclaim the unconditional surrender to the Allied Powers of the Japanese Imperial General Headquarters and of all Japanese armed forces and all armed forces under Japanese control wherever situated.

We hereby command all Japanese forces wherever situated and the Japanese people to cease hostilities forthwith, to preserve and save from damage all ships, aircraft, and military and civil property and to comply with all requirements which may be imposed by the Supreme Commander for the Allied Powers or by agencies of the Japanese Government at his direction.

We hereby command the Japanese Imperial General Headquarters to issue at once orders to the Commanders of all Japanese forces and all forces under Japanese control wherever situated to surrender unconditionally themselves and all forces under their control.

We hereby command all civil, military and naval officials to obey and enforce all proclamations, orders and directives deemed by the Supreme Commander for the Allied Powers to be proper to effectuate this surrender and issued by him or under his authority and we direct all such officials to remain at their posts and to continue to perform their non-combatant duties unless specifically relieved by him or under his authority.

We hereby undertake for the Emperor, the Japanese Government and their successors to carry out the provisions of the Potsdam Declaration in good faith, and to issue whatever orders and take whatever action may be required by the Supreme Commander for the Allied Powers or by any other designated representative of the Allied Powers for the purpose of giving effect to that Declaration.

We hereby command the Japanese Imperial Government and the Japanese Imperial General Headquarters at once to liberate all allied prisoners of war and civilian internees now under Japanese control and to provide for their protection, care, maintenance and immediate transportation to places as directed.

The authority of the Emperor and the Japanese Government to rule the state shall be subject to the Supreme Commander for the Allied Powers who will take such steps as he deems proper to effectuate these terms of surrender.

Signed at TOKYO BAY, JAPAN at 0904 I
on the SECOND day of SEPTEMBER, 1945

重光葵

By Command and in behalf of the Emperor of Japan and the Japanese Government

梅津美治郎

By Command and in behalf of the Japanese Imperial General Headquarters

Accepted at TOKYO BAY, JAPAN at 0908 I
on the SECOND day of SEPTEMBER, 1945,
for the United States, Republic of China, United Kingdom and the Union of Soviet Socialist Republics, and in the interests of the other United Nations at war with Japan.

Douglas MacArthur
Supreme Commander for the Allied Powers

C.W. Nimitz
United States Representative

徐永昌
Republic of China Representative

Bruce Fraser.
United Kingdom Representative

Union of Soviet Socialist Republics Representative

Ed Blamey
Commonwealth of Australia Representative

Dominion of Canada Representative

Provisional Government of the French Republic Representative

Kingdom of the Netherlands Representative

Leonard M. Isitt
Dominion of New Zealand Representative

Surrender Document

The "Instrument of Surrender," signed by the Japanese representatives
aboard the Missouri in Tokyo Bay on September 2, 1945, was drafted by the
Department of War and approved by President Truman. It called for the complete submission
of Japan by the Allied Powers under the command of General Douglas MacArthur.
One copy of the original document was given to the Japanese government.
The other was hand-carried back to Washington, D.C., and
presented to President Truman on September 7, 1945,
in a formal ceremony at the White House. It was later
desposited in the National Archives.

➤ RIGHT, TOP: Japanese Foreign Minister Mamoru Shigemitsu signs the document of surrender aboard the *Missouri*. Leaning over the table to assist him is Toshikazu Kaze, an English-speaking diplomat who studied at Harvard. General Douglas MacArthur is at the microphone and his chief of staff, Lieutenant General Richard Sutherland, is in front of the table. (NATIONAL ARCHIVES) ➤ BOTTOM: Fleet Admiral Chester W. Nimitz signs the surrender papers. Behind him, from left, are General Douglas MacArthur, Admiral William F. Halsey, and Rear Admiral Frederick C. Sherman. (NATIONAL ARCHIVES)

Pen to Paper

General MacArthur used five fountain pens, four black and one red, to sign the official surrender documents. One set of documents was encased in green leather for the United States and the other in black canvas for the Japanese. MacArthur gave two of his black pens to fellow officers and the other two to historical archive collections. The red pen was a gift from his wife and he gave it back to her as a souvenir.

▲ ABOVE, TOP LEFT: A warm hug greets this *Missouri* sailor on the ship's arrival at the Norfolk Naval Station on October 18, 1945. A number of the ship's crew members received their discharge here and returned to civilian life. (NATIONAL ARCHIVES) ▲ TOP RIGHT: Sailors clean camouflage paint from the decks after the surrender ceremony. At the end of their scrubbing sticks are blocks of soft sandstone known as holystones. (NATIONAL ARCHIVES) ▲ BOTTOM: Planes from the Third Fleet carriers fly above the *Missouri*'s forward gun barrels at the conclusion of the surrender ceremony. More than 450 aircraft participated in the fly-over designed to show the Japanese that they no longer ruled the sky. (NATIONAL ARCHIVES)

Korean War

When the North Koreans invaded South Korea on June 25, 1950, the *Missouri* was on a training cruise full of midshipmen from the Naval Academy. The battleship eventually returned to its home port at Norfolk Naval Station, Virginia, where it picked up a new crew, took aboard a large supply of ammunition and headed to the Pacific.

Due to the *Missouri's* fame as the World War II surrender ship, there was a great deal of media interest in its returning to battle. Newspapers and magazines ran stories on the ship and its crew and movie newsreels were produced to document its operations at sea. The Navy also released a recruiting poster featuring an illustration of the ship firing its guns.

After passing through the Panama Canal, the *Missouri* continued west to Hawai'i, where it spent a week undergoing repairs in Pearl Harbor and a day practicing shore bombardment off the uninhabited island of Kaho'olawe. The *Missouri* then threaded its way through the Philippines to Korea, where it joined up with the American and United Nations forces in the Far East commanded by General MacArthur.

MacArthur's strategy became clear when the U.S. First Marine Division and the U.S. Seventh Infantry Division launched an unexpected amphibious assault behind the North Korean front lines at Inchon, the port city of Seoul. The *Missouri's* 16-inch guns blasted the coast and helped drive the enemy north and inland.

On September 21, 1950, five years after MacArthur accepted Japan's surrender aboard the *Missouri* in Tokyo Bay, he made a return visit to the battleship now stationed off Inchon. Two weeks later the *Missouri* became a flagship again upon the arrival of Vice Admiral Arthur D. Struble, commander of the Seventh Fleet.

During its Korean War deployments, the *Missouri* operated out of the naval port at Sasebo, Japan. Due largely to MacArthur's fatherly role, many Japanese now welcomed the Americans.

Victory seemed certain until the Chinese Communists halted the U.N. offensive by sending armies of more than a million troops into Korea. MacArthur responded by asking for more troops to send into China, but this plan led to a public dispute with President Truman, who did not want a protracted war with the Chinese. When MacArthur publicly criticized the U.S. foreign policy, Truman relieved him of all his commands on April 11, 1951.

The Korean War dragged on for another two years before battle lines were stabilized near the 38th parallel. Because the North Korean and Chinese had limited naval air power during the Korean War, the *Missouri* continued shore bombardment without opposition until a truce was signed on July 27, 1953. Truman and MacArthur, whose lives are forever mingled in the history of the *Missouri*, never patched up their differences.

▲ ABOVE: Commander William H. Hoffman, a Navy chaplain aboard the *Missouri*, holds a Roman Catholic service on the fantail of the ship before beginning shore bombardment during the Korean War. (NATIONAL ARCHIVES)

Diplomatic Voyage

*Between the end of World War II and the Korean War, the prestige of the Missouri
as the surrender ship made it a natural choice for diplomatic use. One important duty was to return the
body of the late Turkish ambassador, Mehet Munir Ertegun, from Washington back to Turkey. This mission
led to a postwar U.S. Navy strategy in the Mediterranean region designed to support
democratic governments while containing the Soviet Union.*

▲ ABOVE: The *Missouri*
fires its guns toward
the port city of
Chongjin, North
Korea, in October
1950. This shot of the
battleship in action
was one of the best-
known Navy photos
taken during the war.
(NATIONAL ARCHIVES)

Homemade Flag

⚓

When the Missouri first joined the United Nations fighting force during the Korean War, it was ordered to fly the U.N. flag. Unfortunately, one could not be found. The chief quartermaster collected pieces of fabric, a shipboard artist cut out the pattern, and a tailor from the boatswain's locker stitched it together on his sewing machine. The homemade flag, with its white globe design on a blue background, was ready to fly the next morning.

▲ ABOVE, TOP: The *Missouri* (left) lies moored alongside her sister ship, the *Iowa*, at Yokosuka, Japan, in October 1952. The positioning allowed for easy transfer of flagship staff between ships. (NATIONAL ARCHIVES) ▲ BOTTOM, RIGHT: Hundreds of empty 5-inch powder cases are stacked after a bombardment of North Korea in February 1951. The cases were recycled. (NATIONAL ARCHIVES) ▲ LEFT: Shell casings from the 5-inch guns lie ejected on the deck following a firing at Wonson, North Korea, in March 1953. On March 10 the ship fired a war-high total of 998 rounds. (NATIONAL ARCHIVES) ➤ OPPOSITE PAGE: Crew members catch some rays on the fantail of the *Missouri*. The wings of two floatplanes, sitting on catapults, hang overhead. (NATIONAL ARCHIVES)

The *Missouri* rests at anchor in Tokyo Bay with Mount Fuji rising above the forward gun turrets. The sailor in the foreground was included in the photo taken from another ship. (NATIONAL ARCHIVES)

➤ RIGHT: This U.S. Navy recruiting poster is now a favorite of collectors. Its artwork was based on a photo (see page 41) of the *Missouri* taken in October 1950 during the ship's bombardment of North Korea (U.S. NAVAL INSTITUTE)

Role Model

At the start of the Korean War the Missouri was the only U.S. Navy battleship still in commission. It served as the flagship of the Seventh Fleet and provided gunfire support for the troops ashore while waiting for the Wisconsin to return to service. During the war the Missouri received widespread publicity through photographs, newsreel films and recruiting posters.

Mothball Fleet

If the Missouri seems well-preserved today, it's because it spent much of its life in the Pacific Reserve Fleet at the Puget Sound Naval Shipyard. She was first decommissioned in 1955, returned to active service in 1984, and decommissioned again in 1992 after the Persian Gulf War. During her years in the fleet reserve, the ship was used as background prop in such movies as MacArthur *and the TV miniseries,* Winds of War.

◄ LEFT, TOP: Director Joseph Sargent stages a reenactment of the Japanese surrender ceremony aboard the *Missouri* for the 1977 feature film, *MacArthur*. The ship was moved away from its pier at the Puget Sound Naval Shipyard for the filming. (PUGET SOUND NAVAL SHIPYARD)

◄ BOTTOM: Actor Gregory Peck, standing at the microphones, captures the look and temperament of the famous general in the title role of MacArthur. A Japanese actor bends over the table to sign the surrender document. (PUGET SOUND NAVAL SHIPYARD)

Persian Gulf War

Tomahawks and Harpoons

⚓

The cost to reactivate the Missouri in 1984 was about $475 million. To go along with its 16-inch guns, the ship was modernized with batteries of new Tomahawk and Harpoon missiles that provided an additional offensive punch during the Persian Gulf War. A covered deckhouse was built on the bridge to hold a new generation of sophisticated electronic warfare equipment.

Between the Korean and Persian Gulf Wars the *Missouri* received plenty of rest. Decommissioned in 1955, the battleship spent the next 29 years with the Pacific Reserve Fleet at the Puget Sound Naval Shipyard in Bremerton, Washington. In 1984, the Navy modernized the *Missouri* and it returned to active service as a symbol of American naval power during the Cold War.

Along with its original firepower, the *Missouri* was outfitted with new batteries of long-range, computer-guided Tomahawk and Harpoon missiles. The battleship went on several goodwill missions and was used in the Middle East to protect oil tankers during the Iran-Iraq war.

On August 2, 1990, Iraqi president Saddam Hussein invaded neighboring Kuwait and threatened Saudi Arabia. When Saddam refused to withdraw his troops, the United Nations Security Council authorized the United States and other members to use "all means necessary" to remove Iraqi forces from Kuwait. The U. N. Military Coalition was led by General Norman H. Schwarzkopf, commander of the U.S. Forces.

Prior to the Persian Gulf War, there were top-level Navy discussions to deactivate the *Missouri*. Its sister ships, the *Iowa* and *New Jersey*, were already on their way out. When the Iraqi army took over Kuwait, these plans were canceled and the *Missouri* began preparing for combat.

After the Coalition built up its ground forces in Saudia Arabia, the *Missouri* headed off to its third war and took up a battle station off the island of Bahrain. The *Missouri's* explosive ordnance disposal team spent the first few weeks in the Persian Gulf finding and detonating floating Iraqi mines that were capable of causing serious damage to the ship.

Saddam ignored the U.N. ultimatum to leave Kuwait by January 15, 1991. The Coalition responded with the start of Operation Desert Storm and the *Missouri*, along with its sister Iowa-class battleship, the *Wisconsin*, began pounding Iraq with its Tomahawk missiles and guns. The original World War II plotting computers, now integrated into a modern electronic weapons system, were still able to direct the guns to fire their projectiles with remarkable accuracy.

During Operation Desert Storm, the *Missouri* coordinated the gunfire of all the Coalition ships in the gulf. Coastal surveillance was provided by small, remote-controlled aircraft launched from the *Missouri's* decks. The *Missouri* fired a total of 759 of its 16-inch projectiles during the war.

General Schwarzkopf launched the Coalition's ground forces from Saudi Arabia early in the morning on February 24, 1991. The *Missouri* fired its guns into the occupied territory to fool the Iraqis into thinking there would be an amphibious landing. The ground attack, which came in the opposite direction, resulted in a victory for the Coalition and the liberation of Kuwait.

Eyes in the Sky

During the Persian Gulf War the Missouri *carried a group of remotely piloted vehicles (RPVs) which were launched on reconnaissance missions into enemy territory. These small, high-flying drone Pioneer aircraft, weighing about 400 pounds each, were able to pass over land areas and send back TV images during the day and infrared video at night. This aerial surveillance allowed the ship's crew to hit targets with remarkable accuracy.*

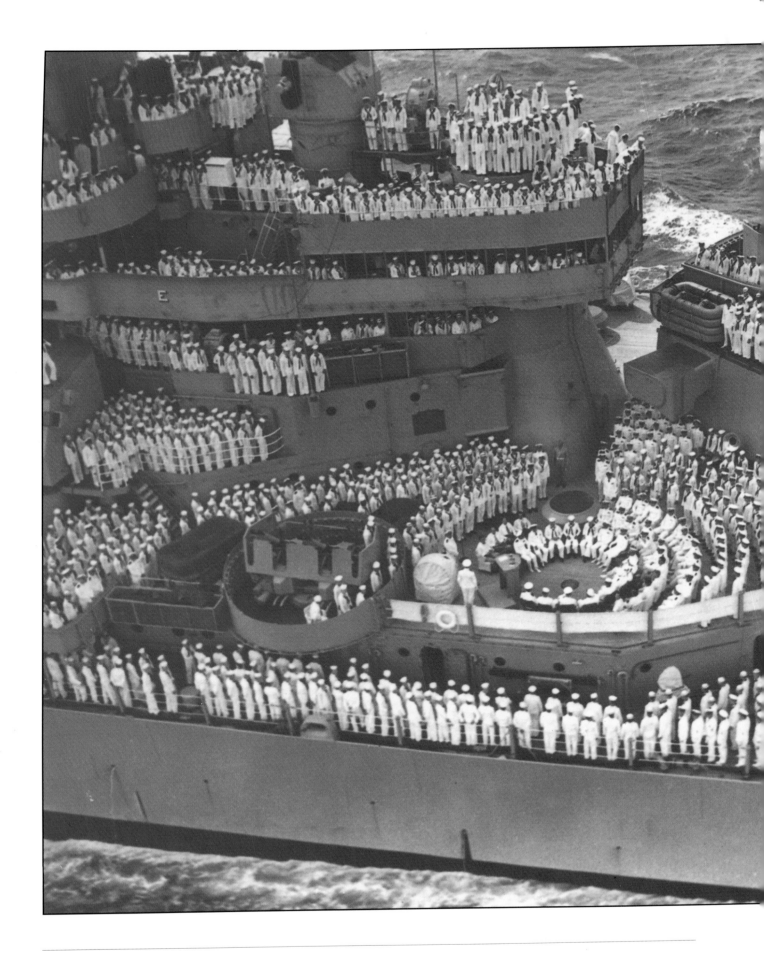

◄ LEFT: Crew members and midshipmen encircle the Japanese surrender plaque on September 2, 1949, to mark the fourth anniversary of the end of World War II. The *Missouri* was en route to Cuba on a training cruise. (NATIONAL ARCHIVES) ▲ ABOVE, TOP: The *Missouri* fulfilled many a sailor's dream in July 1948. During a summer training cruise through the Mediterranean, the ship dropped anchor in the harbor of Villefranche, a town on the French Riviera. (NATIONAL ARCHIVES) ▲ ABOVE, MIDDLE: Navy tugboats spray water in the air to salute the *Missouri* arriving in San Francisco, California, on May 6, 1986. The Golden Gate Bridge is in the background. (NATIONAL ARCHIVES) ▲ ABOVE, BOTTOM: After the Japanese surrender, a decorative map of the *Missouri's* wartime travels was painted on a bulkhead in the officer's wardroom. It has been updated over the years. (NATIONAL ARCHIVES)

Home to Hawai'i

The *Missouri* first steamed into Pearl Harbor on Christmas Eve 1944, to report for duty with the Pacific Fleet. Its last active mission also occurred at Pearl Harbor on December 7, 1991, when the *Missouri* returned to star in the 50th anniversary ceremonies marking the Japanese air attack that propelled America into World War II. Among the guests were several old-time sailors who had escaped from the *Arizona* before it sank.

Secretary of the Navy John Dalton acknowledged the important ties between the *Missouri* and Pearl Harbor on May 4, 1998, when he signed documents transferring the battleship from the Navy to the USS Missouri Memorial Association. Hawai'i's Senator Daniel K. Inouye, a decorated World War II veteran of Japanese ancestry, helped seal the deal.

Less than a month later the ship left the mothballed fleet at Bremerton in Washington's Puget Sound Naval Shipyard and was towed to the resort town of Astoria, Oregon. Here, in the fresh water of the Columbia River, the ship was cleaned of marine organisms that had accumulated on its hull. A week later, the *Missouri* began its final 2,700-mile journey across the Pacific.

Upon reaching Hawai'i, the *Missouri* was towed past the north shore of Molokai. Its tugboat, *Sea Victory*, blew its whistles and the *Missouri* dipped the U.S. flag for the residents of Kalaupapa Peninsula. This friendly gesture continued a Navy tradition begun in 1908, when President Theodore Roosevelt ordered the Great White Fleet to change course and salute the colony of Hansen's Disease patients.

Roosevelt's armada of 16 battleships, known as the Great White Fleet because of their white-painted hulls, included the first USS *Missouri* (BB-11). Sent around the world as a show of U.S. power, the fleet was diverted from its set cruise at the request of Brother Dutton, successor to Father Damien on Moloka'i. The current *Missouri* also saluted the Kalaupapa colony during a visit to Hawai'i in 1986.

More than 25,000 people lined the shoreline as the *Missouri* rounded Diamond Head on Father's Day, June 21, and continued past Waikiki, Ala Moana and Aloha Tower. On the morning of June 22, 1998, the ship was towed into Pearl Harbor and moored at Ford Island's Pier F-5. It will eventually move down the channel to a permanent site on Battleship Row.

Visitors to Pearl Harbor have a unique opportunity to view World War II in the presence of America's two most famous battleships. The USS Arizona Memorial recalls the tragedy that brought America into the war, while the Battleship Missouri Memorial symbolizes the national spirit that rose up in response and ultimately was victorious.

▲ ABOVE: Battleship Missouri Memorial visitors look out from the bridge. Painted below are representations of the ship's service ribbons, which correspond to those worn on an individual's military uniform. (DOUGLAS PEEBLES)

▼ BELOW: The bow of the *Missouri* is pointed respectfully toward the sunken *Arizona*. Many of its crew members are still entombed below.(DOUGLAS PEEBLES)

Movie Plot

Terrorists gain control of the Missouri to hijack its Tomahawk missiles in the 1992 action film, **Under Siege**. Steven Seagal stars as an ex-Navy SEAL who foils the plan. The Navy cooperated with the filming but was less than pleased that the inside man who facilitated the takeover was the ship's executive officer. While the external shots show the Missouri leaving Long Beach on its way to Hawai'i, the interior shipboard scenes were actually filmed aboard the USS Alabama Battleship Memorial in Mobile, Alabama.

Captain's Cabin

There were two cabins for the captain aboard the Battleship Missouri. An in-port cabin, located starboard off the 01 deck, had a bedroom and head, plus an outer room with a writing desk, table, couch and chairs. The state seal of Missouri was painted on a bulkhead. Just aft of the bridge was a smaller cabin used by the captain while the ship was at sea. A separate suite was used as flag quarters whenever an admiral embarked on the ship.

➤ RIGHT, TOP: The *Missouri's* living quarters were spacious compared to earlier battleships. Desk and chairs offered a place to read and write letters home.(DOUGLAS PEEBLES) ➤ BOTTOM: An officer's room below deck. Uniforms were washed and pressed in the ship's laundry. (DOUGLAS PEEBLES)

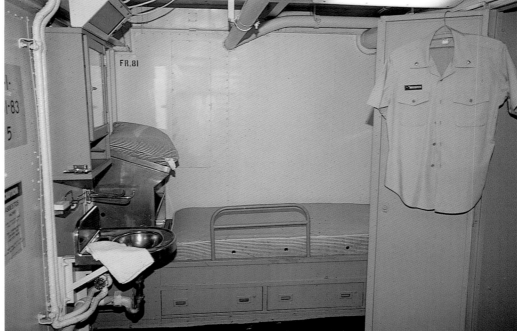

Ship Restoration

Although the Battleship Missouri Memorial is now open to the public, it will take several more years to complete the entire museum. Volunteers, many of them former crew members who served aboard the battleship, will work to remove rust and loose paint, repair metalwork and electrical equipment, refurbish desks and keep up general housekeeping chores. New areas of the ship will be opened as restoration and displays are finished.

Pearl Harbor Selected

It was never a "done deal" that the Missouri would return permanently to Pearl Harbor. Honolulu had to compete with three other U.S. cities—San Francisco, Long Beach, and Bremerton, Washington, to acquire the historic battleship after it was removed from the naval register in 1995. After a lengthy evaluation process, the Navy signed over the ship to the USS Missouri Memorial Association on May 4, 1998.

◄ LEFT, TOP: Holiday menus, postcards, correspondence, and other ship's memorabilia. The *Missouri* had its own print shop below deck. (DOUGLAS PEEBLES)

◄ BOTTOM: A World War II Navy officer's dress whites, sword, and an assortment of commemorative plaques. Hundreds of items have been donated or lent for display by former *Missouri* crew members. (DOUGLAS PEEBLES)

Postal Souvenirs

Mail clerks aboard the Battleship Missouri worked from 5:30 a.m. to midnight on September 2, 1945, processing souvenir letters and cards marking the Japanese surrender ceremony. Each crewmember and guest who witnessed the ceremony was allowed to mail out up to five pieces of mail that day carrying the ship's special postmark. Each person aboard the Missouri also received a wallet-size commemorative card.

Under Tow

The engines of the *Missouri* were silent during its final voyage to Hawai'i in 1998. Moving at 5 knots, it took 29 days for the tugboat Sea Victory to tow the battleship from Bremerton, Washington, to Hawai'i. The well-publicized 2,700-mile trip, which included a week's stopover in Astoria, Oregon, began May 23 and ended June 22, when the ship entered Pearl Harbor. The 415-foot chain and wire towline weighed about 40 tons.

➤ RIGHT: The *Missouri*'s port and starboard anchor chains are 1,080 feet long. Each link weighs 120 pounds. (DOUGLAS PEEBLES)

Ship Aground

The most embarassing incident in the history of the Battleship Missouri occurred on January 17, 1950. While on a daytime voyage out of the Norfolk Naval Station, Virginia, an inexperienced captain drove the ship into a mud flat. The ship remained grounded for two weeks before a team of Navy salvage experts figured out a way to refloat it with the help of the tugboat fleet.

Back to Pearl Harbor

Thousands of Hawai'i residents lined O'ahu's shoreline to welcome the Missouri home on June 21, 1998. After rounding the island of Moloka'i, the ship was towed past Diamond Head, Waikiki Beach, Ala Moana and Honolulu Harbor. As the battleship entered Pearl Harbor, its arrival was announced by traditional Hawaiian conch shell blowers.

Battleship Museums

The Missouri is one of five U.S. battleships now open to the public as museums. The Alabama is in Mobile, Alabama; the Massachusetts is in Fall River, Massachusetts; the North Carolina is in Wilmington, North Carolina and the Texas is in Houston, Texas. Efforts are now underway to find permanent homes for the remaining Iowa-class battleships, the Iowa, New Jersey, and Wisconsin.

▲ ABOVE: All of the *Missouri's* movements and combat operations are controlled from the decks of the superstructure. Tomahawk and Harpoon missile systems were added during a $475 million modernization at the Long Beach Naval Shipyard. (DOUGLAS PEEBLES)

A New Era in the Pacific

A circular bronze plaque, mounted in the teakwood 01 deck of the *Missouri*, marks the spot where World War II came to an end. It was here, on September 2, 1945, in Tokyo Bay that Japanese Foreign Minister Mamoru Shigemitsu signed the official surrender documents that began a new era of peace, respect and stability in the Pacific.

The period between Japan's surprise attack on Pearl Harbor, December 7, 1941, and Japan's surrender nearly four years later, was one of the most momentous in American history. Visitors to the Battleship Missouri Memorial are invited to return to the 1940s to experience first hand what life at sea was like for the men who served on the Navy's last battleship.

Tickets for the *Missouri*, temporarily berthed at Pier F-5, are obtained on shore at the Bowfin Submarine Museum. Guests are then shuttled across the Ford Island Bridge in buses playing radio broadcasts and music popular during World War II. The 1,000-foot pier leading to the battleship features exhibits and memorabilia related to the war years.

Ship tours begin with an orientation in the officer's wardroom off the main deck that includes a film presentation of the ship's history. Visitors may take either guided tours with docents, or self-guided tours.

From the wardroom you may go up to the 01 deck to see the plaque that was installed after World War II to mark the exact spot of the Japanese surrender. This plaque was removed and stored away while the ship was at sea.

Once restored, such areas as the admiral and captain's cabins, engine room, gun turrets, galley, bakery, mess hall, barbershop, sleeping quarters, and sick bay will be open to the public for tours.

You may climb to the main bridge for a panoramic view of Pearl Harbor and today's ships of the Pacific Fleet. It was from here that the captain, protected in the pilothouse citadel by more than a foot of solid steel armor, directed the ship during battle. A ladder leads to the flying bridge, the highest point of the tour.

The bow of the *Missouri* points toward the sunken USS *Arizona*, its crew still entombed below, as a solemn reminder of the supreme sacrifices made by America's sons and daughters during World War II to ensure the new era of freedoms we now take for granted.

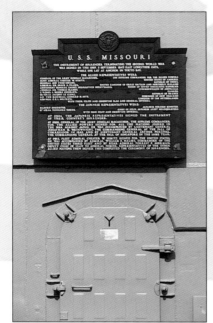

▲ ABOVE: This plaque, hanging above the entrance to the captain's cabin, lists all of the Allied and Japanese representatives who participated in the Japanese surrender ceremony. (DOUGLAS PEEBLES)

▼ BELOW: Sea trials off the coast of southern California following the *Missouri*'s return to active service in 1986. Navy veterans were assigned to teach battleship operations to the younger sailors. (U.S. NAVAL INSTITUTE) ► FOLLOWING PAGES: The Battleship Missouri Memorial in Pearl Harbor opened to the public on January 29, 1999. Together with the Arizona Memorial, it is one of Hawai'i's most popular attractions. (GARY HOFHEIMER)

Permanent Mooring

The Missouri *is temporarily berthed at Ford Island's Pier F-5. This pier was originally built for the battleship in 1988, when the Navy planned for it to join the Pacific Fleet at Pearl Harbor. In several years, the* Missouri *will be moved permanently to a new location on Battleship Row.*

➤ RIGHT, TOP: The *Missouri's* 16-inch guns are no longer operational. A plug keeps the barrel clean and guards against accidents. (DOUGLAS PEEBLES) ➤ MIDDLE: A close-up view of the *Missouri's* superstructure. The battleship's main bridge provides a panoramic view of Pearl Harbor. (DOUGLAS PEEBLES) ➤ BOTTOM: A view of the *Missouri* from the visitor shuttle. The ship is now tied to Ford Island's Pier F-5, about 300 yards from the Arizona Memorial. (DOUGLAS PEEBLES)

When the Missouri was towed into Pearl Harbor on June 22, 1998, it wasn't quite ready for prime time. The ship's gray paint was faded, scrape marks marred the hull and the teak decks were beginning to crack. Rust spots were everywhere. After an SOS call went out for help, a work force of 5,000 volunteers donated their talents and more than 25,000 hours of time to get the Battleship Missouri Memorial shipshape in time for its grand opening on January 29, 1999.

◄ LEFT: Visitors on the main deck of the *Missouri*. The average self-guided tour takes about one hour. (DOUGLAS PEEBLES)

The First Missouri

The present Missouri (BB-63) moored at Pearl Harbor was not the first great battleship named for the "Show Me" state. An earlier Missouri (BB-11) was commissioned in 1903 and remained in service until 1919. It was one of the legendary battleships that comprised the Great White Fleet sent around the world in 1908 by President Theodore Roosevelt to show off U.S. naval power.

Ship's Statistics

USS Missouri (BB-63)
Type
Iowa-class battleship

Sister Ships
USS Iowa
USS New Jersey
USS Wisconsin

Dimensions
Total length: 887 feet, 3 inches
Length at waterline: 860 feet
Maximum beam: 108 feet, 2 inches
Height: 209 feet, 8 inches
Draft at full load: 37 feet, 9 inches

Displacement
Standard: 45,000 tons
Full load: 57,500

Maximum Speed
33 knots

Boilers
Eight 600 PSI Babcock and Wilcox

Engines
Four General Electric Turbines

Tank Capacity
Fuel oil: 2.5 million gallons
Aviation fuel: 30,000 gallons
Water: 239,000

Primary Battery
Guns: Nine 16-inch, 50-caliber, three triple turrets

Projectiles: armor-piercing, 2,700 pounds; high-capacity, 1,900 pounds
Powder: Standard load, six 110 pound bags
Rage of fire: Two rounds per minute, per gun
Range: 23 miles

Secondary Battery
Guns: Twelve 5-inch, 38-caliber, in six twin mounts after modernization (originally 20 guns in ten twin mounts)
Projectiles: 55 pounds
Powder: 30 pounds
Rate of fire: 15 rounds per minute, per gun
Range: 9 miles

Weaponry (After 1984-86 modernization)
Four Vulcan/Phalanx 20mm Gatling guns capable of firing 50 rounds per second against aircraft and missiles
Four Harpoon anti-ship missile canisters (16 missiles)
Eight Tomahawk missile launchers (16 missiles)

Armor
Hull beltline: 13.5 inches thick
Turret faces: 17 inches thick
Second deck: 6 inches thick
Conning tower sides: 17.3 inches thick

Propellers
Two inboard (five blades, 17 feet, 5 inches)
Two outboard (four blades, 18 feet, 3 inches)

Rudders

Two, 340 square feet in area

Anchors

Two, port and starboard bow, each
    weighing 30,000 pounds
Each anchor chain is 1,080 feet long
Each link weighs 120 pounds

Mechanics

Two inboard propellers (five blades, 17 feet,
    5 inches)
Two outboard propellers (four blades,
    18 feet, three inches)
Two rudders
Eight boilers
Four steam turbines

Anchors

Two, each weighting 30,000 pounds

Personnel

World War II: 134 officers, 2,400 enlisted
Korean War: 114 officers, 2,070 enlisted
Persian Gulf War: 66 officers, 1,500 enlisted

➤ RIGHT: Pulleys for the hawser cable, which
is used to moor the ship to the pier. (DOUGLAS
PEEBLES)

Brief Chronology

January 6, 1941
Keel laid at New York Navy Yard

December 7, 1941
Pearl Harbor attacked by Japanese aircraft

January 29, 1944
Launched at New York Navy Yard

June 11, 1944
Commissioned at New York Navy Yard

December 24, 1944
First visited Pearl Harbor

February-March, 1945
Supports carrier airstrikes against Tokyo, the invasion of Iwo Jima and airstrikes against Okinawa

April 11, 1945
Hit by Japanese kamikaze plane

September 2, 1945
Japan formally surrendered on 01 deck

January17, 1950
Runs aground out of Norfolk Naval Station

September, 1950
First shore bombardments during Korean War

February 26, 1955
Decommissioned at Puget Sound Naval Shipyard

May 10, 1986
Recommissioned at Puget Sound Naval Shipyard

January 16, 1991
Participates in Operation Desert Storm

December 7, 1991
Visits Pearl Harbor for 50th anniversary of Japanese attack

March 31, 1992
Decommissioned at Long Beach Naval Shipyard

March 31, 1992
Decommissioned for second time at Long Beach Naval Shipyard. Towed to Bremerton, Washington

May 4, 1998
Navy transfers ownership to USS Missouri Memorial Association

May 23, 1998
Towed from Bremerton, Washington

June 21, 1998
Arrives off Diamond Head

June 22, 1998
Enters Pearl Harbor

January 29, 1999
Grand Opening of Battleship Missouri Memorial, 55 years to the day after original launch

▲ ABOVE: The Battle-
ship Missouri Memo-
rial adjacent to Ford
Island in Pearl Harbor.
In the water at the
upper right is the
Arizona Memorial.
(GARY HOFHEIMER)